Searchlights for Spelling
Year 4 Photocopy Masters Book

Chris Buckton   Pie Corbett

CAMBRIDGE
UNIVERSITY PRESS

Introduction

Searchlights for Spelling is a comprehensive spelling scheme for Years 2–6/Primary 3–7 that covers all the word-level spelling objectives of the National Literacy Strategy (NLS) and meets the requirements of the National Curriculum.

How to use this book

This photocopy masters book contains a range of photocopiable material to support the:
1. tracking and assessment of progress;
2. provision of homework to support the units in the scheme;
3. reinforcement and revision of the spelling teaching.

Tracking progress

The Teacher's Book for Y4 contains a full scope and sequence chart which shows objectives and coverage in all components. This book also includes a Tracking sheet (see pages 3–5) which provides spaces for you to comment on children's performance and progress across the 18 core units (and 3 additional units) in Y4. Copies of this sheet can be used to record spelling marks taken from the dictations, as well as information about specific areas of difficulty or observations of progress.

A copy of the dictation sentences for Units 1 to 18 is reproduced (pages 7 and 8), with target test words highlighted. This can be used in the form of a spelling 'running record', to show individual performance in each test, and to help identify areas of strength and weakness. The sentences can also be given to children, to help them revise or reinforce learning (this should probably happen when children have completed the year's units, as these words are the test words for the whole year). The dictations for the additional units are also provided.

A list of Key words taken from the *Searchlights* list of words to learn and the list of oddbods, taken from the NLS medium-frequency word lists for Years 1 and 2, is also given on page 6. These can be used as appropriate, as a reminder for children or to help you track progress.

Assessment

Three SATs-style cloze procedure tests are provided (pages 10–12) to support the objectives covered through the year, and to give children valuable practice in spelling under test conditions. One test is provided for each term, but you may wish to use them at different times. For these tests, children need their own copy of the test passage. To support delivery and marking of the tests, completed versions of the test passages are included on page 9. (See the Teacher's Book, page 6 for more information about using and marking these tests.)

To help children to assess their own progress, two self-assessment sheets are provided. A set of 'I can…' targets (page 14) related to the Y4 objectives are provided: children colour a star to show they have met the target, and write in a date. A second sheet provides a list of additional statements relating to strategies for spelling (page 15). Both of these formats can be used in group or individual discussion, as part of target-setting and self-assessment.

Revision

Six revision photocopy masters provide further support, and can be used as necessary for individuals and groups, either in class, or as homework. Brush-up games on pages 45–46 offer additional quickfire ideas to use in class, to reinforce spelling objectives little and often.

Spelling log

A format for a spelling log is included on page 13, to be filled with words as appropriate. Children may already have a log of some kind, in which lists of words are kept. This format offers one model which can be copied and made into a small book. *Searchlights* actively promotes the building of word lists to support children in analysing and remembering spell iings.

Spelling tips

This book also contains useful summaries of spelling strategies (Having problems spelling a word?, page 16; Learning new words, page 17). These can be given to children to keep, display and annotate to build their own useful records and as a resource for spelling in writing. These sheets also appear in the reference pages of the Pupil's Book (pages 46–48).

Homework

A worksheet is included for each of the 18 core units (PCMs 1–18), and 3 additional units (PCMs AU1, AU2 and AU3). These photocopy masters provide reinforcement or revision related to the unit, and opportunities for investigations. Each PCM also contains a list of Words to learn for the unit and these words form part of the dictation test. These words are differentiated into three levels (A, B and C) to be allocated appropriately. (See the Teacher's Book, page 6 for more information.)

Information for parents/carers

How to help your child with spelling (pages 47–48) gives a useful summary of approaches to learning spelling. This can be sent home to support children's learning of words, and can provide a focus for home–school links in the area of spelling. The guidance is designed to make parents and carers feel actively involved in their child's progress in spelling.

Tracking sheet

Names	Unit 1	Unit 2	Unit 3	Unit 4	Unit 5	Unit 6	Unit 7					
	To spell two-syllable words with double consonants	To distinguish between the spelling and meanings of common homophones	To spell regular verb endings	To spell irregular tense changes.	To recognise and spell suffixes al, ary and ic	To change nouns and adjectives into verbs by the use of suffixes	To recognise and spell the suffixes ship, hood, ness, ment					
	NLS 4.1.W5	NLS 4.1.W6	NLS 4.1.W7	NLS 4.1.W8	NLS 4.1.W9	NLS 4.1.W14	NLS 4.1.W9					

Tracking sheet, continued

Names	Unit 8	Unit 9	Unit 10	Unit 11	Unit 12	Unit 13	Unit 14					
	To add suffixes to words ending in **f**	To spell words with common endings	To recognise and spell prefixes beginning with <u>a</u>	To recognise and spell common prefixes	To explore the occurrence of certain letter strings	To explore the occurrence of certain letters	To spell words with common letter strings but different pronunciations					
	NLS 4.2.W5	NLS 4.2.W6	NLS 4.2.W7	NLS 4.2.W7, W8	NLS 4.2.W4, W8 4.3.W5	NLS 4.3.W5, W3, W4	NLS 4.3.W6					

Tracking sheet, continued

Names	Unit 15	Unit 16	Unit 17	Unit 18	Additional Unit 1	Additional Unit 2	Additional Unit 3						
	To collect and classify words with common roots	To practise extending and compounding words through adding parts	To recognise and spell the suffixes ible, able, ion (tion/sion)	To form diminutives	To identify mis-spelt words and develop spelling strategies	To use a range of suffixes to make adjectives and investigate spelling patterns	To revise common contractions; to distinguish *its* and *it's*						
	NLS 4.3.W7	NLS 4.3.W8	NLS 4.3.W9, W3, W4	NLS 4.3.W12	NLS 4.3.W1, W2, W3	NLS 4.3. W3, W8	NLS 4.3.W10						

Key words – words to learn in Searchlights Y4

activate	chiefs	express	I'm	mortgage	right	think
additional	cleaned	extract	I've	motivate	rough	threw
admit	clock	eye	imaginative	mourn	route	tight
advance	clumsiness	fairness	interval	movement	rudely	towards
adventure	collection	fare	interview	moving	rushed	tractor
adverb	competition	February	introduction	musical	sea	traditional
affordable	confusion	finalise	invention	mustn't	selfish	traffic
align	contract	fistfight	invitation	mystery	shocking	trick
almighty	cough	flies	January	national	shopped	trough
almost	could	flour	journey	necessary	shopping	twin
alone	couldn't	flow	kerb	octopus	shouldn't	unable
already	cracker	follow	kettle	otter	show	unknown
also	crept	foolish	kitchenette	overflow	shutting	unplug
although	deafen	forcible	kite	overheat	silliness	untidy
altogether	decorative	fought	kitten	overlap	silly	used
apologise	departure	fright	knife	overrun	sipped	valuable
argumentative	describe	funnily	knives	overtake	sleepily	walk
around	dictionary	funny	leaf	patted	slight	walking
asleep	didn't	glorify	leaflet	payment	smallish	warm
ate	digital	glove	leaves	peace	sorry	washable
attractive	discuss	gloves	library	pickle	speckled	watching
awake	disgrace	gone	life	playful	spectacular	we'll
away	diskette	gosling	lighten	pleasure	spectator	we've
bare	dismiss	government	lives	plough	spoke	wept
basic	division	greediness	loving	popped	spotlight	white
beautiful	dizziness	greedy	make	popping	strode	wicked
beech	dough	grow	manuscript	postpone	submit	wife
began	dramatic	happiness	memorise	pour	suggestion	window
better	drank	happy	microbe	powerful	suitable	winner
beware	dries	hare	microchip	prescribe	sulk	wives
bite	dropped	having	microphone	prevention	supervision	wizard
blink	drove	he'll	microscope	puppy	suspicious	wolf
bough	duckling	height	microwave	purify	swallow	wolves
bought	encourage-	helpfully	milk	rabbit	swam	won't
breakable	ment	herd	miniature	racing	swift	wonderful
broken	energetic	hippo	minibus	recount	swim	word
brought	enjoyment	historic	minimum	reddish	swing	would
butted	enough	hole	miniskirt	refreshing	swoop	wrote
came	enviable	horrible	miserable	respectable	swore	you'd
can't	environment	horrific	misplace	rested	take	you'll
carrot	every	hospital	moisture	reversible	terrorise	you've
chief	everything	hour	mortal	rhythmic	thankful	

Oddbods – medium frequency words

across	change	guess	stopped	there	thought
any	different	half	suddenly	they're	told
asked	don't	might	sure	think	under
being	electricity	other	their	though	until

© Cambridge University Press 2002   Searchlights for Spelling Y4

Dictation sentences (Units 1–18)

Full details of how to use the dictation sentences appear in the Teacher's Book (page 6).

Unit 1
OB Bad weather **stopped** the football match.
A The brown **rabbit** was hopping round the garden.
My father said that I must not be **silly**.
B My friends all love my new **puppy**.
A **hippo** is not as large as an elephant.
C "I'm **sorry** that I can't come on Sunday," said Joy.

Unit 2
OB The children left all of **their** carrots.
A A **hare** is like a big rabbit.
The bus **fare** to town is one pound.
B My sister and I often go swimming in the **sea**.
The sleepy kitten opened one **eye**.
C I **threw** the ball into the garden next door.

Unit 3
OB I **asked** Mum if I could have a baby rabbit.
A The happy hippo was **walking** by the sea.
Dad was **watching** us through the window.
B The fast cars were **racing** round the town.
John **rested** for a while by the sea.
C She **sipped** the cool, clear water.

Unit 4
OB I **thought** the otter in the sea looked happy.
A The little boy **began** to pat the puppy.
Last term we **swam** at school.
B Bill **wrote** such a funny story at school today.
Jane and Ben **ate** four fish from the sea.
C Dad **drove** to town and did the shopping.

Unit 5
OB My mother **told** me not to be silly.
A The **musical** boy sang a song for us.
At Christmas we eat **traditional** food.
B On the first of **January** it was cold and wet.
The church in our town is very **historic**.
C Unfortunately Jim is unwell and is in **hospital**.

Unit 6
OB For a **change** we had cake and ice-cream for tea.
A We had to **memorise** some words from the dictionary.
Those boys always **terrorise** the other children.
B Jan was sorry and wanted to **apologise**.
Jeff had to **purify** the water before he sipped it.
C In February I will give you an **invitation** to my birthday party.

Unit 7
OB The children stopped **being** silly right away.
A **Fairness** is very important in sport.
Liz was told off for her **silliness**.
B Sally found **happiness** with her new friends.
Everyone should look after the **environment**.
C My **selfish** brother doesn't know how to share.

Unit 8
OB The invitation said that we should come at **half** past four.
A They say cats have nine **lives**.
A cook needs to have lots of **knives**.
B My brothers both have new **wives**.
The scary **wolves** terrorise everyone in the wood.
C I went shopping to get a better pair of **gloves**.

Unit 9
OB "I **might** come too after I have rested for a while," said Dad.
A You will look silly if your trousers are too **tight**.
The pop star was caught in the **spotlight**.
B The little brown rabbit took a **bite** of the carrot.
Pete could fly a **kite** very well.
C The wind blew harder and the sea got very **rough**.

Unit 10
OB We haven't got **any** additions this week.
A The thief worked **alone** in the night.
Sue **also** has a bad cough.
B Those boys have got into a fight **already**.
The bright light keeps me **awake**.
C My puppy is foolish but full of **adventure**.

Unit 11
OB "I will keep walking **until** I get home," said Fran.
A You should **unplug** the light before you go to bed.
I'm sorry that my room is always so **untidy**.
B The bath was too full and started to **overflow**.
Dan's racing car is going to **overtake** Sue's.
C In hospital they **prescribe** pills to help you get better.

Unit 12

OB Can you **guess** what colour my new kite is?

A If something is too **warm** it can overheat.
Pam had a bad leg and was unable to **walk**.

B The children were walking **towards** the library.
You must **beware** of the wolves in the dark wood.

C A **swift** and a swallow are both birds.

Unit 13

OB Pat's sister went through the door and **across** the room.

A Cold weather can **make** you cough.
I will **take** my brother to play on the swing.

B The wizard did another good **trick**.
Dad's **clock** had stopped working.

C Jim's mum gave me some **milk** and a **cracker**.

Unit 14

OB **Though** it was cold, the sun was very bright.

A The ball went right through the broken **window**.
Please could you **show** me where the hospital is?

B I **would** like to apologise for my clumsiness.
Sam's **journey** began as soon as it was light.

C "Do you think I have **bought** enough cake?" asked Mum.

Unit 15

OB Ned was **sure** he would be the winner of the competition.

A An **octopus** lives in the sea and has eight legs.
The journey takes an hour by **express** bus.

B Mr Brown uses a **tractor** to plough his land.
Pat read an **extract** from the book's introduction.

C The show we went to see last week was **spectacular**.

Unit 16

OB My new book describes lots of **different** animals.

A The baby drank the warm milk **sleepily**.
John made a suggestion **helpfully**.

B The school play this year was **wonderful**.
The twins lived in an **attractive** house.

C Shopping is fun and gives me a lot of **pleasure**.

Unit 17

OB **Suddenly** Tom turned around and ran away quickly.

A Mum bought me a dress that was **suitable** for school.
I feel sad and **miserable** today.

B Mum's attractive ring is very **valuable**.
The wonderful book that I want is almost **affordable**.

C The horrible traffic jam brought a lot of **confusion**.

Unit 18

OB I'm wearing a suitable miniskirt **under** my coat.

A The boys sat sleepily in the back of the **minibus**.
The **leaflet** described the important new invention.

B A **gosling**, a kitten and a puppy are all baby animals.
That **microscope** is not suitable for children.

C The class was working with **minimum** supervision.

Additional Unit 1

OB We played a football team from the **other** division.

A The brothers were **having** a terrible fight.
The duckling was **loving** its big adventure.

B Mum **shopped** for hours and bought a new microwave.
Ann **dropped** the doll out of the window into the garden below.

C The wizard was full of **mystery** and tricks.

Additional Unit 2

OB Many inventions use **electricity**.

A Jen's new microscope is more **powerful** than her old one.
Mum's ring is valuable and **beautiful** too.

B Dad put the kettle on to make a **refreshing** drink.
Greedy Jim began to sulk as there was no cake left.

C Joe watched the **suspicious** man walking through the park.

Additional Unit 3

OB **Don't** stay awake too late at night.

A **You've** been very energetic this morning.
I've stopped being silly at school.

B I think **we've** rested for long enough now.
He'll have to overtake that car if he wants to win.

C You **mustn't** postpone doing your homework.

Termly SATs type tests

The following tests are designed to provide SATs practice each term. The words selected focus on the term's objectives or on key words and oddbods.

To be useful, spelling tests should always be diagnostic. Look carefully at the results to find out what strategies the children are using. Do not penalise them for intelligent, plausible guesses. Take account of the term's objectives and any special focus (how well they have learnt the oddbods, for example) and also note whether they are retaining objectives taught earlier in the year (for instance, if they spell a prefix correctly). You could award two marks for each word: one mark if the target phoneme or letter pattern is spelt correctly and a second mark if the whole word is spelt correctly.

Term 1

Two-syllable words with double consonants; homophones; regular verb ending <u>ed</u>, irregular verb tenses; suffixes <u>al</u>, <u>ic</u>.

<u>Bobby</u> felt <u>happy</u> when he <u>knew</u> he could <u>buy</u> a <u>new</u> pet. He went to the <u>local</u> pet shop <u>by</u> the <u>traffic</u> lights. They had a lovely <u>puppy</u> and a <u>kitten</u>, but he wanted a <u>rabbit</u>. They had so many and he <u>tried</u> to <u>choose</u>. In the end he <u>chose</u> a brown one. But when he <u>took</u> it home, it made a <u>hole</u> in its cage and <u>swallowed</u> a <u>whole</u> pack of <u>butter</u>. He decided to take it back to the shop.

"Could I <u>change</u> it?" he <u>asked</u>. "I'd like a snake instead."

Term 2

Common endings <u>ight</u>, <u>tion</u>, <u>ough</u>; prefix <u>al</u>; letter strings <u>wa</u>, <u>ss</u>.

You <u>might</u> <u>already</u> know quite a lot about the <u>serious</u> problem of <u>pollution</u>. It <u>affects</u> us all. I'm <u>sure</u> you sometimes <u>worry</u> about the <u>environment</u> being spoiled, <u>although</u> maybe you don't know what to do about it. If <u>enough</u> of us wrote to the <u>government</u>, we <u>ourselves</u> could help to <u>save</u> <u>lives</u>. <u>Also</u>, <u>I</u> <u>guess</u> we could improve the <u>water</u> if we <u>watched</u> what was happening to our rivers. We're not <u>helpless</u>. Let's fight, and hope for <u>success</u>!

Term 3

Letter strings <u>wa</u>, <u>wo</u>, <u>ss</u>; word endings <u>ough</u>, <u>ight</u>; suffixes <u>ing</u>, <u>ion</u>, <u>ic</u>, <u>ible/able</u>; <u>it's/its</u>; compound words.

Dear Governors

I am <u>writing</u> to draw your <u>attention</u> to a serious problem. The <u>traffic</u> on the road outside our school is <u>terrible</u>. <u>Although</u> it is <u>slightly</u> <u>less</u> busy since the <u>bypass</u> was <u>built</u>, it has not improved <u>enough</u> to be <u>crossable</u> at the beginning and end of the day.

The <u>worst</u> place is by the school drive. Parents park by <u>its</u> main gates when children are <u>swarming</u> out of the <u>building</u>.

Could parents be told that <u>it's</u> <u>preferable</u> to stop at the top of the road, away from the school? I <u>wonder</u> if it is also <u>possible</u> to ask <u>everyone</u> to consider whether they <u>might</u> walk or bike to school?

Yours sincerely

A school pupil

① Pet problems

practice

_____ felt _____ when he

_____ he could _____ a

_____ pet. He went to the _____

pet shop _____ the _____ lights.

They had a lovely _____ and a

_____, but he wanted a _____.

They had so many and he _____ to

_____. In the end he _____ a brown

one. But when he _____ it home, it made

a _____ in its cage and _____

a _____ pack of _____. He decided

to take it back to the shop.

"Could I _____ it?" he _____.

"I'd like a snake instead."

1 ◯   2 ◯

3 ◯   4 ◯

5 ◯   6 ◯

7 ◯   8 ◯

9 ◯

10 ◯   11 ◯

12 ◯

13 ◯   14 ◯

15 ◯

16 ◯   17 ◯

18 ◯   19 ◯

20 ◯   21 ◯

(2) Pollution

You _____ _____ know quite a lot

about the _____ problem of _____ .

It _____ us all. I'm _____ you

sometimes _____ about the _____

being spoiled, _____ maybe you don't know

what to do about it. If _____ of us wrote

to the _____ , we _____ could help

to _____ _____ . _____ ,

I _____ we could improve the _____

if we _____ what was happening to our

rivers. We're not _____ . Let's _____ ,

and hope for _____ !

practice

1 ◯ 2 ◯

3 ◯ 4 ◯

5 ◯ 6 ◯

7 ◯ 8 ◯

9 ◯

10 ◯

11 ◯ 12 ◯

13 ◯ 14 ◯ 15 ◯

16 ◯ 17 ◯

18 ◯

19 ◯ 20 ◯

21 ◯

③ A letter to the school governors

Dear Governors,

I am _____ to draw your _____

to a serious problem. The _____ on the road

outside our school is _____. _____

it is _____ _____ busy since the

_____ was _____, it has not

improved _____ to be _____ at the

beginning and end of the day.

The _____ place is by the school drive.

Parents park by _____ main gates when

children are _____ out of the _____.

Could parents be told that _____ _____

to stop at the top of the road, away from the school?

I _____ if it is also _____ to ask

_____ to consider whether they

_____ walk or bike to school?

Yours sincerely

A school pupil

practice

1 ◯ 2 ◯

3 ◯

4 ◯ 5 ◯

6 ◯ 7 ◯

8 ◯ 9 ◯

10 ◯ 11 ◯

12 ◯

13 ◯

14 ◯ 15 ◯

16 ◯ 17 ◯

18 ◯ 19 ◯

20 ◯

21 ◯

Searchlights for Spelling Y4

Spelling log sheet

Name ....

Date ....

Spelling log

Look Say Cover	Write Check	Try again?

Fold here

You can use this to help you. Cover the word list.

Fold the page along the dotted line.

Look at each word and **Say** it out loud.

Then **Cover** the list before you **Write** the word.

Open up the page to **Check**.

If it isn't right, **Try again**. Underline the tricky bit.

Name .... Date ....

Can you . . . ?

	Yes!	Date
I can spell words from the word list.	☆	
I can use knowledge of prefixes and suffixes when spelling.	☆	
I can spell words that end in vowels other than <u>e</u>.	☆	
I can spell most plurals.	☆	
I can spell words using prefixes and suffixes such as <u>in</u>, <u>im</u>, <u>ir</u>, <u>il</u>, <u>pro</u>, <u>sus</u>, <u>auto</u>, <u>bi</u>, <u>trans</u>, <u>tele</u>, <u>circum</u>, <u>cian</u>, <u>ful</u>.	☆	
I can use word roots and derivations to spell, e.g. <u>sign</u>, <u>signature</u>, <u>signal</u>, <u>signify</u>.	☆	
I can spell pronouns, e.g. <u>their</u>, <u>our</u>, <u>your</u>.	☆	
I can distinguish and spell common homophones, e.g. <u>ate</u>, <u>eight</u>.	☆	
I can double the consonant (after a short vowel) in such words as <u>big</u> – <u>bigger</u>.	☆	
I can use an IT spell-check.	☆	
I can drop the <u>e</u> when adding <u>ing</u>.	☆	
I can keep the <u>e</u> when adding a suffix that starts with a consonant, e.g. <u>lovely</u>.	☆	
I can use the rule for 'i before e' and common exceptions.	☆	
I can spell words that end in <u>y</u> when they change their form, e.g. <u>fly</u> – <u>flies</u> – <u>flying</u>.	☆	
I can transform words by tense (<u>hop</u> – <u>hopped</u>), by comparison (<u>better</u> – <u>best</u>), by negation (<u>clear</u> – <u>unclear</u>).	☆	

Searchlights for Spelling Y4

Do you . . . ?

Do you . . . ?	Yes!	Date
I try to spell words I am not sure about.	☆	
I listen to and sound out the separate sounds in a word.	☆	
I break words up into syllables to make spelling easier.	☆	
I use rhyme or the meaning of a word to help me spell.	☆	
I look for words within a word.	☆	
I use common prefixes and suffixes.	☆	
I practise **Look Say Cover Write Check**.	☆	
I jot down words and look at them to check that they are spelt correctly.	☆	
I look for common errors in my writing and keep notes in my spelling log.	☆	
I look up words in a dictionary or word book.	☆	
I use the apostrophe to show when letters are missing and to show that something belongs to someone.	☆	
I can spell common words that sound the same but look different (e.g. to, too, two).	☆	
I can spell two-syllable words that contain double consonants.	☆	
I can spell words that contain the same spelling pattern but which sound different.	☆	
I can add suffixes to words ending in **f**.	☆	
I use my knowledge of grammar to help spell verb endings like s, ed and ing.	☆	
I use any spelling rules I've learned.	☆	
I use different spelling strategies.	☆	
I think of a word with a similar pattern.	☆	
I look at my mistakes and try to find out what I've done wrong.	☆	

Having problems spelling a word?

Try these . . .

- What sounds can you hear? Which letters could spell each sound?
- Think of another word that rhymes with that word.
- Break the word into syllables. Remember, every syllable has a vowel or a y in it.

  fly has one syllable   *fly/ing* has two   *but/ter/fly* has three
- Think of words with the same sort of pattern, e.g. true, blue.
- Think of words with similar meanings, e.g. ear, hear, heard.
- Are there any prefixes or suffixes?
- Is there a rule that you know, e.g. what happens when you add ing?
- Is there a mnemonic? e.g. there is a hen in when.
- Use a dictionary or spellchecker.
- Work with a spelling partner.
- Ask a friend.
- Have a go!
- Underline the word and check it later.
- Never dodge a useful word – have your best go and keep writing!
- When you make a mistake, have a look at it and think about why you've made it. This will help you to put it right.

Your spelling log

Start a spelling log. This will help you to remember the words you need to learn.

These are some of the things you can put in your spelling log.

- Lists of words you often get wrong;
- ways to remember tricky words;
- things you have learnt about spelling;
- words to learn for the week;
- homophones;
- irregular past tense spellings;
- investigations;
- word collections (e.g. words with a prefix, words with common endings);
- prefixes, suffixes;
- useful spelling tips, e.g. when you add ing to a word ending in an e, drop the e.

Learning new words

Practise **Look Say Cover Write Check**.

Look

- Look at the shape of the word.
- Make a picture of the word in your mind.
- Look at the letter patterns that make up each sound.
- Break the word into syllables.
- Look for words within the word.

Say

- Say the whole word.
- Say the beginning sound.
- Say the end sound.
- Say the middle part of the word.
- Say the letter names.
- Say the whole word again.
- Over-pronounce any parts that you might forget.

Cover

- Cover the word.
- Picture the word in your mind.
- Hold it in your mind as if it's on a TV screen.

Write

- Write the word in joined writing.
- Think about the picture in your mind as you write.
- Say the letter names or the sounds.

Check

- If it isn't right yet, try again!
- Think about why you got it wrong.
- Look at the tricky bits.
- Underline the tricky bits.

Name ....

Date ....

Alphabet doubles

Apple

Make an alphabet of two-syllable words containing two consonants. The first three are done for you.

a	is an <u>apple</u>	j		s	
b	is a <u>battle</u>	k		t	
c	is <u>coffee</u>	l		u	
d		m		v	
e		n		w	
f		o		x	
g		p		y	
h		q		z	
i		r			

EXTRA CHALLENGE

Can you find any two-syllable words with double vowels?

Write them here.

Which vowels don't double?

Words to learn

A funny	silly	rabbit	follow		**ODDBOD**	
B happy	puppy	hippo	carrot	kitten	stopped	
C shopping	swallow	better	sorry	otter		

Searchlights for Spelling Y4

Name _____   Date _____

Beat the riddler

Solve these riddles.

In agony? _____

Windows have them. _____

   If you shout too much. _____

   Gee up! Clippetty clop _____

A metal _____

Robbers do this. _____

   Take a quick look. _____

   Top of a mountain. _____

Quiet _____

A small bit of pie. _____

   Juicy to eat _____

   Two of them _____

Strong men have them. _____

Eat these from the seashore
– but cook them first! _____

✗ EXTRA CHALLENGE

Now write a riddle of your own.

_____

_____

_____

_____

_____

_____

_____

_____

_____

_____

_____

_____

Words to learn

Ⓐ bare   hare   fare

Ⓑ sea   eye   flour   beech

Ⓒ right   peace   herd   threw   hole

ODDBODS

their

there they're

Name _____

Date _____

Change ends!

Beware of the two catch-you-outs!

   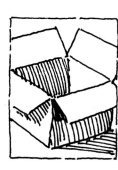 

sail	bark	box	open	fly
sailing	_____	_____	_____	_____
sailed	_____	_____	_____	_____
sails	_____	_____	_____	_____

shake	fry	fish	kiss	whistle
_____	_____	_____	_____	_____
_____	_____	_____	_____	_____
_____	_____	_____	_____	_____

EXTRA CHALLENGE

Now do the same for the verbs <u>die</u> and <u>dye</u>.

Words to learn

A watching walking shutting moving **ODDBOD**

B popped rushed cleaned rested racing asked

C used popping patted sipped butted

Searchlights for Spelling Y4

Name ....   Date ....

Then and now

Finish the chart about what you did as a baby and
what you do now.
Add two more verbs and descriptions.

Verb	Then	Now
crawl	I crawled because I couldn't walk!	I crawl through the tunnel.
throw		
sing		
feed		
sleep		
wear		
speak		
eat		
bite		

Words to learn

A began	came	drank	swam		**ODDBODS**
B wrote	ate	wept	crept		think
C brought	strode	gone	drove	spoke	thought

Name ....

Date ....

Personal wordsearch

Make your own wordsearch for <u>al</u>, <u>ary</u> and <u>ic</u> words.

Begin with these words.

```
                                        A
                                        N
                                        G
                                        E
                                        L
                                        I
        S   U   P   E   R   S   O   N   I   C
```

EXTRA CHALLENGE

<u>Picnic</u> ends with a <u>c</u> and <u>trick</u> ends with a <u>ck</u>.

Find other words that end with a <u>c</u> or a <u>ck</u>.

Try to work out the rule.

Words to learn

Ⓐ musical   traditional   additional   national   **ODDBOD**

Ⓑ January   February   historic   necessary   horrific   told

Ⓒ dictionary   traffic   rhythmic   hospital   library

Name ....

Date ....

Specialise in suffixes!

Change these adjectives and nouns into verbs by using one of these suffixes.

ise	_en_	_ify_	_ate_

soft _____   elastic _____   moisture _____

glad _____   ideal _____   electric _____

real _____   mad _____   pollen _____

simple _____   clear _____   summary _____

 EXTRA CHALLENGE

What did you have to do to the spelling of the nouns and adjectives?
Complete this chart with the words you had to change.

Word	+ suffix	Drop letters / add extra letters / other

Name .... Date ....

Specialise in suffixes!

Change these adjectives and nouns into verbs by using one of these suffixes.

ise	en	ify	ate

soft _____

glad _____

real _____

simple _____

elastic _____

ideal _____

mad _____

clear _____

moisture _____

electric _____

pollen _____

summary _____

EXTRA CHALLENGE

What did you have to do to the spelling of the nouns and adjectives?
Complete this chart with the words you had to change.

Word	+ suffix	Drop letters / add extra letters / other

Name ....   Date ....

Specialise in suffixes!

Change these adjectives and nouns into verbs by using one of these suffixes.

ise	_en_	_ify_	_ate_

soft _____   elastic _____   moisture _____

glad _____   ideal _____   electric _____

real _____   mad _____   pollen _____

simple _____   clear _____   summary _____

EXTRA CHALLENGE

What did you have to do to the spelling of the nouns and adjectives?
Complete this chart with the words you had to change.

Word	+ suffix	Drop letters / add extra letters / other

Words to learn

A memorise   terrorise   activate   motivate   **ODDBOD**

B purify   apologise   lighten   deafen   glorify   change

C invention   invitation   suggestion   introduction   competition

Name ....

Date ....

Adding suffixes

Add the right suffix to each word.

Choose from these suffixes:

| dom | like | ish | some | ment | ness | ship |

fit _____   war _____

announce _____   champion _____

free _____   partner _____

wicked _____   life _____

tidy _____   self _____

fool _____   king _____

silly _____   retire _____

loathe _____   tire _____

EXTRA CHALLENGE

Put the words you have made into pairs, like this.

treatment + pavement

· ·

Words to learn

Ⓐ movement   enjoyment   fairness   silliness   **ODDBOD**

Ⓑ environment   government   happiness   greediness   dizziness   being

Ⓒ selfish   foolish   reddish   smallish   clumsiness

    Searchlights for Spelling Y4

Name ....   Date ....

Half and half

Write these sentences in the plural.

I wear a scarf and a glove. _____

The calf was safe from the wolf. _____

_____

From the _____ f floating on the sea.

_____

_____

Write these

The dragons

The calves ate leaves. _____

The stories were about the lives of thieves. _____

_____

EXTRA CHALLENGE

Write one more sentence using words ending in **f** for each set.
Then change the sentence in the same way as before.

_____

_____

_____

Words to learn

A knife	knives	life	lives			**ODDBOD**
B wife	wives	wolf	wolves			half
C leaf	leaves	chief	chiefs	glove	gloves	

Name .... Date ....

Call it a day!

It is easy enough to spell the days of the week.
They all end in <u>day</u> and have a capital letter.
But do you know where the names came from?
Match the days of the week to their origins.

Sunday	named after the Norse god Odin (Woden)
Monday	named after the Norse goddess Frigg
Tuesday	named after the Roman god Saturn
Wednesday	'day of the sun' (Anglo-Saxon)
Thursday	named after the Norse god of war, Tiw
Friday	named after the Norse god of thunder, Thor
Saturday	'day of the moon' (Old English)

EXTRA CHALLENGE

Find out where the names of the months of the year came from.

· ·

Words to learn
Ⓐ tight   fright   slight   spotlight   **ODDBOD**
Ⓑ white   bite   kite   height   fistfight   might
Ⓒ although   rough   enough   cough   trough

Name

Date

Class rules!

Write some class rules using as many words with the <u>al</u> prefix as possible.
Here are some words to start you thinking.

Always . . .   We almost . . .   Although . . .

Rules

EXTRA CHALLENGE

How many <u>al</u> words can you find in the dictionary? Which ones have
an <u>al</u> prefix (try to work it out from their meaning and pronunciation:
<u>al</u> stems from <u>all</u>).

Words to learn

Ⓐ alone   away   also   almost   **ODDBOD**

Ⓑ already   adverb   admit   around   awake   any

Ⓒ almighty   advance   although   adventure   asleep   altogether

Name ....   Date ....

Prefix word wheel

Cut out the two circles of card.

Join them together in the centre with a paper fastener.

Turn the wheel to make some words.

List the words on a piece of paper.

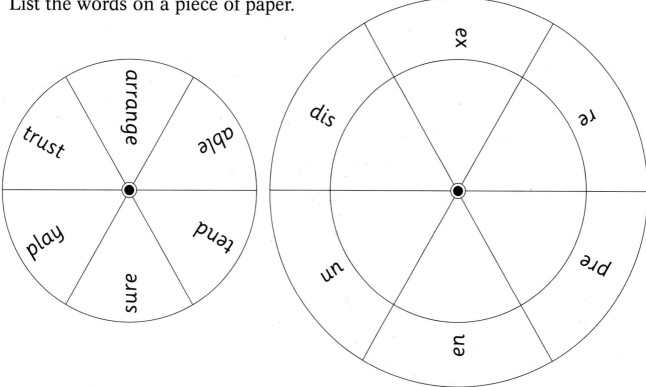

 EXTRA CHALLENGE

Now work out and write down the meanings of the words on your list.

Words to learn

A untidy   unplug   unknown   unable   **ODDBOD**

B overflow   overheat   overlap   overrun   overtake   until

C interview   prescribe   postpone   submit   interval

© Cambridge University Press 2002   Searchlights for Spelling Y4

Name ....

Date ....

Warbling words

Read the <u>wo</u> and <u>wa</u> tongue twister.

Worried wolves with wonderful warm woolly waistcoats wouldn't walk through the wood without wobbling.

Try saying it as fast as you can.

Now make up your own tongue twister from <u>wo</u> and <u>wa</u> words.

```



```

 EXTRA CHALLENGE

How many different sounds can <u>wo</u> make? Make a list.

Words to learn

Ⓐ walk   warm   word   swore   **ODDBOD**

Ⓑ towards   beware   swim   swoop   wicked   guess

Ⓒ swing   wizard   twin   winner   swift

Name ....   Date ....

Investigating letter strings with l

What other consonants can go with l?

You should be able to find six consonant clusters.

Write words for each cluster.

Here's one to start you off.

bleed					

EXTRA CHALLENGE

Which other consonants can follow l at the end of a word?

Make a list of words.

Words to learn

A take   make   kettle   kerb   **ODDBOD**

B trick   clock   sulk   think   blink   across

C broken   milk   cracker   speckled   pickle

Name ....   Date ....

gh investigation

Make some lists of gh words.

- Words where gh sounds like **f** (like laugh)

  _____

  _____

- Words spelt ough (like though)

  _____

  _____

- Words spelt augh (like caught)

  _____

  _____

- Words spelt igh (like light)

  _____

  _____

Do you notice any patterns?

EXTRA CHALLENGE

Can you find words where gh has a different sound (not **f**)?

Words to learn

					ODDBODS
A show	flow	grow	window		
B would	mourn	pour	journey	hour	though
C bought	plough	bough	fought	dough	through

Name ....

Date ....

Look for the Latin

Here are some Latin root words.

Can you think of two words for each root?

aqua – water _____ _____

annus – year _____ _____

decem – ten _____ _____

unus – one _____ _____

EXTRA CHALLENGE

Write down some words which come from the Latin roots <u>bene</u> (= well)
and <u>male</u> (= ill).

Words to learn

Ⓐ misplace   recount   express   octopus   **ODDBOD**

Ⓑ extract   tractor   contract   mortal   mortgage   sure

Ⓒ spectacular   spectator   describe   manuscript   finalise

Name ....

Date ....

Automatic adjectives?

A way of making adjectives is by adding <u>ic</u>.

Sometimes the ending is <u>otic</u>, <u>atic</u> or <u>etic</u>.

Collect words ending in <u>ic</u>. Sort them into sets.

Here are some to start you off.

energetic

neurotic

automatic

terrific

Do you notice any spelling patterns? _____

_____

Find out what the words mean.

EXTRA CHALLENGE

Make a list of four words with suffixes that you think are very tricky
to spell. Make sure you've got them right and then test your family
or friends!

For example:

Is it independ<u>ant</u> or independ<u>ent</u>?

Respons<u>ible</u> or respons<u>able</u>?

Words to learn

Ⓐ *funnily*   *sleepily*   *helpfully*   *rudely*   **ODDBOD**

Ⓑ *attractive* *decorative* *thankful*   *wonderful*   *playful*   *different*

Ⓒ *pleasure*   *departure*   *moisture*   *encouragement* *payment*

Name

Date

Test your family or friends!

Make a list of 10 words that have _ible_ and _able_, or _ion_ (_tion_, _sion_) endings.
Use the words from the work you have done so far in class.

Ask your family or friends to have a go at spelling them.

Which ones did they find difficult?

If they got them right, how do they remember which is which?

Then test yourself, using **Look Say Cover Write Check**.

Words to learn

Ⓐ horrible   reversible   suitable   miserable   **ODDBOD**

Ⓑ valuable   affordable   respectable   forcible   enviable   suddenly

Ⓒ confusion   division   supervision   collection   prevention

Name

Date

Huge homework

Find as many words, prefixes and suffixes
as you can which mean 'large'.
Ask your family or friends to help you.

 EXTRA CHALLENGE

Which of the words above have prefixes or suffixes?

. . . .

Words to learn

A minibus   leaflet   duckling   kitchenette   **ODDBOD**
B microscope gosling   diskette   microchip   miniskirt under
C minimum   miniature microwave   microphone microbe

Name .... Date ....

Spelling questionnaire

Find an adult or older brother or sister who will answer these questions.

How do you rate yourself as a speller?

_____

What do you do when you don't know a spelling?

_____

What words do you find tricky?

_____

What do you do to remember any tricky words?

_____

How were you taught spelling at school? Did it help?

_____

EXTRA CHALLENGE

Repeat the questionnaire with other people you know and see how their answers compare.

Did you learn anything new from any of their answers?

• •

Words to learn

A having   loving   flies   dries   **ODDBOD**

B every   could   route   shopped   dropped   other

C everything   mystery   disgrace   dismiss   discuss

Name .... Date ....

Spot the change

All of these words can be made into adjectives by adding a suffix.

Which have to change their spelling? Sort them into two sets.

Give examples of adjectives.

enjoy   fantasy   horrify   graph   irritate
agree   recognise   plenty   dread   envy

Don't change	Example	Change	Example

EXTRA CHALLENGE

Can you make some adjectives out of nouns by adding these word endings?
Make at least three for each ending.

<u>ly</u>   <u>some</u>   <u>al</u>

Words to learn

A powerful   beautiful   washable   breakable   **ODDBOD**
B dramatic   energetic   basic   refreshing   greedy   electricity
C suspicious   shocking   argumentative   digital   imaginative

Name ....

Date ....

Contraction Snap

Complete each pair of cards. Then cut them out and use them to play snap
or pelmanism.

✂

I am	I'm
I have	
who is	
she had	
he will	

✂

was not	
are not	
can not	
will not	
there is	

 EXTRA CHALLENGE

Add some more pairs of words and their contractions to your set of
snap cards.

Words to learn

Ⓐ I've   I'm   you've   you'll   **ODDBOD**

Ⓑ we'll   can't   he'll   you'd   we've   don't

Ⓒ mustn't   shouldn't   won't   didn't   couldn't

    Searchlights for Spelling Y4

Name _____   Date _____

Word sort <u>ing</u>

Add <u>ing</u> onto these words and sort them into three groups.

bat _____   move _____

come _____   rip _____

cry _____   rush _____

cut _____   shake _____

do _____   slip _____

hoot _____   stare _____

jump _____   take _____

like _____   tap _____

look _____   write _____

just add <u>ing</u>	drop the <u>e</u>	double it

Name ....

Date ....

Word sort plurals

Make these words plural and sort them into four groups.

army _____   jelly _____

chair _____   man _____

child _____   mouse _____

class _____   number _____

fax _____   race _____

fly _____   rich _____

foot _____   six _____

frog _____   snail _____

hutch _____   tooth _____

add s	add es	change y to i	odd ones

© Cambridge University Press 2002   Searchlights for Spelling Y4

Name .... Date ....

Muddled compounds

Read this short story. Sort out the muddled compound words.

weekend
Last endweek Sam visited her parentsgrand. On daysun

morning she was eating fastbreak with her mothergrand.

They were tucking into a fruitgrape when they heard a noise.

It was bodysome or thingsome tapping by the bindust. Sam

rushed longhead and fell over. She hurt herself and was looking

at a torn nailfinger when she saw what had been making the

noise. It was a somehand frog trying to eat an wormearth.

As soon as it saw Sam it leapt onto the boardcup and across

the boardside. It even tried to jump stairsup. Sam chased it.

Mothergrand screamed. "This is not a groundplay. Stop playing

with that frog before your fathergrand comes stairsdown and

sees it." At that moment the frog played frogleap out of the

window. Sam leaped like a keepergoal but it

was too late. Her somehand prince was gone!

Name ....

Date ....

Silent letters

Draw lines between rhyming pairs of words.
Underline any silent letters in red.

knife	calm
caught	know
chalk	life
crumb	numb
dumb	reel
eight	home
farm	talk
folk	taught
gnome	thumb
show	weight
kneel	yolk

TIP

To help you remember how to spell words with silent letters try saying
the silent letters as if you could hear them.

Name ....

Date ....

Our teacher, Mr Nasty

Change the meaning of this speech by adding <u>un</u> or <u>dis</u> to some of the words.

Mr Jones is our teacher. Our class find him very *unfriendly* friendly. We

think that he is the most pleasant teacher that we have had.

He is popular with everyone in the school because he is kind

and fair. He has made us all very happy this year and we

think that we are lucky to be in his class.

He likes us all and we make sure that we obey him at all times.

Usually our class is very tidy and a place of great order. There

is a bond of trust between us. We try hard to please him at all

times and make sure that we are always honest. We agree with

everything that he says.

Name ....

Date ....

The long and the short

Complete the empty boxes.

you are	you're
	he's
	we're
they are	
I will	
we have	
	you've
	won't
let us	
shall not	
have not	
	tell 'em
	won't
	I'd
could not	
	aren't
does not	
	it's
there is	

Searchlights for Spelling Y4

Brush-up Games

The following guided group/whole class activities are designed to revise and reinforce important objectives from Year 3. See also ALS Module 4.

1 Find a verb

NLS spelling objective: 3.1.W8: adding <u>ing</u>

- Start with a verb beginning with <u>a</u>, e.g. *acting*.
- Go through the alphabet, taking turns to say a word ending in <u>ing</u>.
- Who can spell their word? Children write and show their spellings on dry-boards.
- Recap rules for dropping final <u>e</u>.

2 Scramble

NLS spelling objective: 3.1.W9: spelling pattern <u>le</u>

- Write tickle, bubble, candle and table on the board.
- Identify the pattern and remind the children about common endings.
- Then scramble the spelling of *prickle*, *apple*, *muddle* and *handle* (and possibly *vegetable* as a challenge) – and write the anagrams on the board.
- Pairs work on dry-wipe boards to unscramble the anagrams.

3 Quickwrite endings

NLS spelling objective: 3.1.W8: and handwriting W20 (see ALS module 4 page 18)

- Demonstrate writing <u>ing</u> on the board, saying the letters and pointing out the joins.
- Say a verb with an <u>ing</u> ending, e.g. *playing*.
- Children practise writing it, paying particular attention to the joins.
- Children suggest other verbs.
- Repeat for <u>ed</u> endings and common suffixes.

4 All Change

NLS spelling objective: 3.2.W1: 'long' vowel phonemes; 3.2.W20: joined handwriting

- Write the starting word on the board, e.g. *meet*, demonstrating handwriting joins.
- Read it aloud together, segmenting and then blending the phonemes.
- Get up and Go: children take it in turns to change one letter to make a new word, e.g. *meat*.
- Say the new word aloud, segmenting and blending as before.
- Continue at a lively pace until ideas run out.

5 Make a word

NLS spelling objective: 3.1.W10 and 3.1.W11: common prefixes

- On the board or on small cards, write a selection of adjectives and verbs, e.g. *build*, *pay*, *obey*, *code*, *lucky*, *tidy*, *usual*, *pare*, *fix*, and prefixes e.g. <u>un</u>, <u>de</u>, <u>dis</u>, <u>re</u>, <u>pre</u>.
- Children take it in turns to make a new word, e.g. *decode*.
- Keep a list of all the words they find.
- Practise writing some of them, paying attention to handwriting joins.

6 Word shapes

3.2.W6: using visual skills

- Display a list of selected key words with different outline shapes, e.g. could, where, very.
- Draw outline shapes of key words on the board, showing the number of letters and any ascenders or descenders.
- Children take it in turns to write the word which fits an outline.
- Cover the word and everyone spells it on dry-wipe boards.

7 Key word quiz

NLS spelling objective: 3.2.W3: to recall high frequency words learnt in KS1

- Give the children clues for words chosen from NLS list 1, e.g. *another word for 'once more' (again)*, or *this word begins with d̲ and ends with r̲ and you can you open it (door)*.
- Children race to solve the clue and spell the word.
- Volunteers take it in turns to make up clues for the rest of the class.

8 Missing apostrophe

NLS spelling objective: 3.3.W15

- On the board, write a list of shortened forms with the apostrophes missing, e.g. *dont, cant, doesnt, hasnt, Ive, wont, theres, Ill*.
- Get up and Go: children take turns to come out and put in the apostrophe (make a dramatically large one backed with blu-tak).
- Can they write the long version? Check that they understand that the apostrophe stands for the missing letters.

9 Hidden words

NLS spelling objective 3.3.W8: short words within longer words

- Write the word something on the board.
- In pairs, children write down as many words within the word as they can find, e.g. *so, some, me*.
- Do the same activity using children's names.

10 Mind the Gap!

NLS spelling objective: 3 3.W1: identifying 'long' phonemes

- On the board or on small cards, write some words with initial and final consonants and a gap in the middle, e.g. *l_d, b_l, g_t, b_n*.
- Children take turns to suggest vowel phonemes to fill the gap.
- Add a catch-you-out by including a split digraph e.g. *b_n_*.

How to help your child with

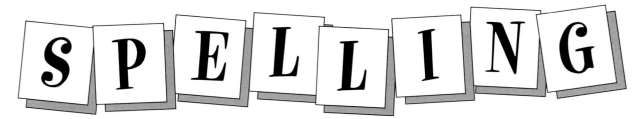

The reason for learning to spell is so that we can write. Give your child plenty of purposeful opportunities to write, for example:

- holiday scrapbooks;
- letters to relatives, or for free offers;
- messages and notices around the house;
- notes and cards to friends and relations;
- helping to write shopping lists, notes, reminders, etc.;
- writing own stories or information booklets.

Make sure they have some pencils, paper and blank writing books. To help them with spelling you can:

- play sound games like 'I spy with my little eye';
- make up nonsense rhymes together;
- play games like *Hangman*, *Boggle* and *Scrabble*;
- supply them with a spelling if they get stuck;
- discuss spelling patterns, rules and exceptions;
- buy a simple, hand-held spellchecker. These usually have games such as *Anagrams*.

As they develop, children will see many more patterns in words and, by Year 4 have an understanding of some spelling rules. However, because there are so many patterns to learn it takes several years to become an accurate speller. Most adults still have difficulty with some words, no matter how many times they have used them.

Words are fascinating! Help your child to enjoy and explore them. Spelling shouldn't be a boring slog. It's about thinking, not just memorising lists of words.

- Point out interesting differences in the way sounds are spelt.
- Work out the rules together by investigating different spellings.
- Help your child to make lists of rhyming words.
- Collect words from newspapers, magazines and catalogues.
- Do simple crosswords together.
- Look for words within longer words (letters must be consecutive, e.g. <u>ark</u> within <u>park</u>ed).

- Look for 'word families'. Some are similar because of the spelling pattern, e.g. b<u>eat</u>, <u>f</u>eat, <u>tr</u>eat, <u>wh</u>eat. Some are related in terms of meaning, e.g. *sign, signal, signature.*
- Look at common endings and beginnings, e.g. <u>ly</u>, <u>ing</u>, <u>ed</u>, <u>s</u>, <u>es</u>, <u>un</u>, <u>im</u>, <u>dis</u>
- Look at words which sound the same but are spelt differently (e.g. *pear/pair*).
- Practise making words for smaller versions of particular objects, by using the endings <u>ette</u>, <u>let</u>, and <u>ling</u> and the beginnings <u>mini</u> and <u>micro</u>.

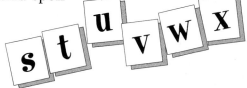

- Give lots of praise for good guesses.
- Never nag about incorrect spellings. Try and find out what bit of the word is causing the problem.
- Offer praise for the bits that are right, and help your child to figure out what they're doing wrong – this will help them to correct their mistakes.
- Practise little and often.
- Talk about spellings you or your child find hard to remember, and make up ways of getting them right.
- Share tricks for remembering words, e.g. *'There's <u>a rat</u> in sep<u>a</u>r<u>a</u>te'.*
- Break long words down into smaller bits and spell a piece at a time.
- Chant difficult spellings.
- Notice spellings that share patterns.
- Have fun – or it's not worth doing!

Paired spelling

Some children find spelling very difficult. If your child is struggling then it could be helpful to spend 10 minutes every day following this simple procedure to support them in learning their individual lists (between 5 and 15 words at a time). Ask your child to explain the rule, pattern or spelling strategy that is being learned.

LOOK SAY COVER WRITE CHECK

- Child reads the word/says it aloud/spells (or chants) the letters out/ tries to spell it out without looking.
- Discuss 'tricky bits' and devise a way of remembering them.
- Repeat this several times before attempting writing if child finds it hard to remember.
- You cover the word.
- Child writes it down.
- Check – if incorrect, revisit two or three more times.

Keep up this routine. It can help to have a regular time every day. Give this as much importance as 'hearing reading'. Spelling does lie at the root of writing, and a little bit every day will help your child to become a better speller and therefore to find writing easier.

Searchlights for Spelling Y4